THE FLEET AIR ARM AND ROYAL NAVAL AIR SERVICE IN 100 OBJECTS

DAVID MORRIS

AMBERLEY

First published 2019

Amberley Publishing
The Hill, Stroud
Gloucestershire, GL5 4EP

www.amberley-books.com

Copyright © David Morris, 2019

The right of David Morris to be identified as
the Author of this work has been asserted in
accordance with the Copyrights, Designs and
Patents Act 1988.

ISBN 978 1 4456 8902 9 (print)
ISBN 978 1 4456 8903 6 (ebook)

British Library Cataloguing in Publication Data.
A catalogue record for this book is available from
the British Library.

Origination by Amberley Publishing.
Printed in the UK.

INTRODUCTION

Every service or working organisation has its own specific equipment, methods, ethos and traditions. These are often the result of many years of development and expansion that in time define that particular service for what it is and how it operates. This book uses a selection of objects to portray how the Royal Navy has expanded over more than a century to include aviation as a key part of its operational requirement, the impacts this has had, and how the service has adapted and responded as a result.

The Royal Navy has always been at the forefront of innovation, new ideas and technology that it can explore and use to improve its advantage at sea. When the Wright Brothers achieved the first manned powered aircraft flights in 1903, the Royal Navy did not miss the importance this very significant event, and although it would be another seven years before the Navy adopted its own full aircraft flying programme, the stage was set to explore naval aviation, even in its most basic form.

Grown from the early, precarious determination to take the first flimsy aircraft to sea more than a century ago to today's supercarriers carrying whole squadrons of supersonic aircraft, it is easy to assume perhaps that the Royal Navy's flying activities are limited purely to operations from or closely associated with its ships. In reality the story is far broader, and covers a truly global range of responses, whether it is combat, defence or humanitarian aid. Since the First World War, naval aviation has been utilised to support ground forces in areas as diverse as the Western Front in Europe and the deserts of Gallipoli. A century later the Fleet Air Arm still trains for and operates across any climate range and geographical situation. From Arctic waters and mountains to desert and jungle environments, the Fleet Air Arm is at a constant state of readiness to respond where and when required.

The Royal Navy's aviation timeline is marked with numerous first achievements, objects, devices and inventions, many of which would be adopted by the navies of other countries or aid technical development in other areas. Flying from ships takes not only skill and courage from the aircrew, but also demands the best, most robust and failsafe technology. Royal Navy aircraft have to be engineered to the highest level of safety: there are no convenient airfields to divert to at sea if an emergency or mechanical failure occurs. In such a situation the outcome and options are limited if your aircraft is not in the most reliable flying condition.

It also requires the engineers and maintenance crews to be trained to the highest level. This builds a natural team working spirit, and life among the whole crew of an aircraft carrier at sea becomes the life of a tight-knit community, which continues when the crews disembark to their respective land-based air stations, or stone frigates as they are occasionally known.

The Navy has long been steeped in traditions and customs, and adding a new community of naval aviators to this has brought with it a spread of new traditions, activities and disciplines. This has not been restricted solely to the working environment, but has also crossed into leisure and recreational areas that have spawned many new games and activities specific to the Royal Navy and Fleet Air Arm. With this mix of new technologies, working practices and recreational pursuits has also come a whole new language. Names, phrases, nicknames, descriptions, sayings (some more repeatable than others!), abbreviations, calls, signals and even general speech are laced with a vocabulary that takes time to learn and understand and is unique to the Royal Navy, the Royal Naval Air Service and the Fleet Air Arm.

The 100 subjects chosen to depict this hopefully capture the spirit, essence, achievements and history of naval aviation from its earliest beginnings to the world-leading position the Royal Navy holds today.

Although only a snapshot of information per subject, this book hopefully includes an interesting spread of the obvious and also some more unusual objects and subjects that define the service and identify the various and at times unique ways in which the Navy operates aircraft. It has been a difficult task to decide what to include or sadly leave out, but hopefully the selection will prompt readers to see or think differently about the objects that are included.

1. The Crow's Nest

Mounted high up the mast of a ship, the observation turret or platform has long been referred to as the crow's nest, a clear reference to those sharp-eyed avians who choose to nest and perch in the highest positions to maintain a good lookout over their surroundings. Providing a clear view of the surrounding area and an extended view over the horizon at sea is critical for effective reconnaissance, observation and information-gathering. Any rise in height at sea will immediately provide an improved view in terms of distance beyond the horizon. Standing at sea level the view to horizon is only 5 km (3 miles). Raise yourself to 30 meters in height and the distance you can see increases to 20 km (13.5 miles). In many ways, the start point for naval aviation begins in the crow's nest, and the desire to not only increase its height above the ship, but ultimately seek to detach it and move it many miles away, returning with valuable information from far beyond the horizon.

2. Man-Lifting Kites and Kite Balloons

Above, below and opposite: In 1908, with manned flight still in its infancy and with an effective shipborne aeroplane still more than two years away, the Royal Navy was nevertheless keen to explore ways of getting a man airborne over the deck of a ship at sea, and to a greater height than the ship's crow's nest observation platform would enable.

Tethered balloons, carrying a man in a basket, and man-lifting kites were trialled to explore the possibilities and capabilities of raising an observer aloft, winched up from the deck of a moving ship, utilising the slipstream for lift. In these early years, American Wild West showman, inventor and aviation pioneer Samuel Franklin Cody worked closely with the Royal Navy, experimenting with his bat-winged, man-lifting kites. Although restricted by weather and wind conditions, ascending kites to viewing heights of 150 m (492 feet) could be achieved in good conditions. Such elevated positions could allow views over the horizon of up to 43 km (27 miles).

3. Airships

Airships played an important role in naval aviation even though their first venture with His Majesty's Airship No. 1 (known as *Mayfly*) ended in disaster. A freak storm and strong gusts of wind caused the craft to beak in two on its launch day, 24 September 1911. *Mayfly* was not just an airship, it was a statement to the rest of the world that Britain was as very much at the forefront of aviation, and on an impressive scale. Despite the disastrous setback of *Mayfly*, many smaller rigid and semi-rigid airships were successfully built and utilised by the RNAS throughout the First World War, providing a useful, manoeuvrable observation vehicle for Royal Naval use at sea. Initially tethered to a ship and hoisted by means of a winch, the airship would develop into a free-flying aircraft that could be used for reconnaissance, submarine-spotting and light bombing duties at sea. Classes of airship were identified by their role and/or construction method: C = Coastal patrol; NS = North Sea; SS = Sea scout; R = Rigid; and SR = Semi-rigid construction. The RNAS used 162 airships during the First World War and much of the post-war civilian airship industry benefitted greatly from the Royal Navy's experiences with these machines.

4. Lantern from Naval Airship No. 9

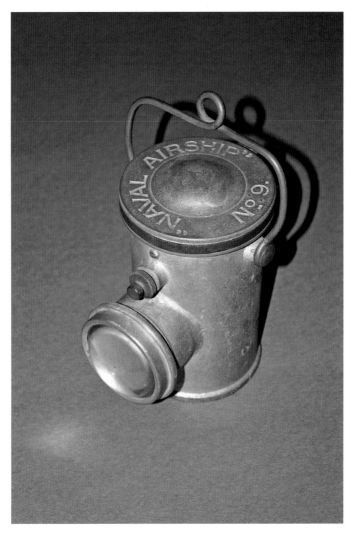

To the casual observer, this small, ordinary-looking lantern appears to be little more than a hand lamp that belonged to Naval Airship No. 9, as its lid clearly indicates. However, its design is significant to the environment it was destined to be used in: that of an airship filled with highly inflammable hydrogen gas. Naked lights or candle lamps would have been disastrous in close proximity to a gas-filled airship, let alone on board, so a safe battery lantern had to be created. Weight was also a consideration, so the main body of the lamp being constructed in aluminium keeps the lamp's weight down. The handle is formed from thick brass wire, but critically both materials have been chosen as metals that will not cause a spark should the lamp be accidentally jarred against a hard surface. The lens is a thick orb of toughened glass that would not smash easily should the lamp be dropped. The lid retaining the battery is screwed securely into place, making the lamp watertight and keeping the battery and internal components securely protected. A well-insulated Bakelite switch completes this stylish little lamp that belies its ultra-safe construction.

5. Cat Mascot

Ships and aircraft that carry the number or code 13 have long been feared to be jinxed. To dispel the bad luck a black cat (in some form) would be carried on board. In the First World War, RNAS Airship No. SS-13 was considered by its crew to need such a good luck charm, and so a small stuffed toy black cat mascot was carried on all flights. The good luck charm must have worked as Airship SS-13 became the longest-serving airship with the RNAS.

6. Francis McClean

Opposite below and above: By 1910, wealthy businessman and keen aviator Francis McClean was working closely with the growing number of Britain's pioneer aircraft manufacturers. Purchasing land at Eastchurch on the Isle of Sheppey, Kent, to create a flying field, McClean became a leading figure in the Royal Aero Club of Great Britain, and personally made two aircraft available to the Royal Navy to aid its embryonic flying training programme. McClean, who had gained a Royal Aero Club flying certificate in 1910, joined the RNAS in August 1914, initially being put in charge of aerial coastal patrol work, but later becoming a Flying Instructor at the RNAS experimental flying field on the Isle of Grain, Kent. Without the generosity of this far-sighted individual it is unlikely that the Royal Navy's flying programme would have been as advanced as it was by the outbreak of the First World War.

7. Royal Flying Corps Naval Cap Tally

This cap tally ribbon dates from pre-1914, when the Royal Flying Corps was Britain's only recognised military flying service, within which was contained a naval flying wing. This cap ribbon predates the identification of the RNAS as an individually named organisation and captures that brief period in time when someone could be issued with a Royal Flying Corps ribbon but be in the naval wing and conducting naval flying duties.

8. The Royal Naval Air Service – The RNAS

By 1908 the British Government (under Prime Minister Asquith) was sufficiently interested in aviation to appoint a committee within the Imperial Defence Committee to investigate flying for military purposes. The committee included officers from the Army and the Navy and initially amalgamated the requirements of both services. With Murray Sueter (pictured above) taking the role of the Director of the Admiralty Air Department in 1912, more emphasis was placed on the specific requirements of naval aviation and its development. A central flying school was established at Upavon in Wiltshire for both services to use, and soon to follow was the Royal Navy's own experimental flying fields at sites based at Eastchurch on the Isle of Sheppey in Kent, and on the Isle of Grain, situated a short distance away on the Hoo Peninsula. The joint military flying programme continued to expand and on 13 April 1913, by Royal Warrant, the Royal Flying Corps (RFC) was established as an official military flying organisation, including a naval wing within its structure. However, the Navy would soon demonstrate that its flying and training requirements were sufficiently different to warrant the formation of its own specific service, and on 1 July 1914 the RNAS was formed.

9. RNAS Cap Badge – Fleet Air Arm Cap Badge

Opposite above: To better establish an identity between the Royal Flying Corps and the newly forming RNAS, an individual badge insignia was determined to be necessary. A first version by graphic design artist Eric Gill featured an anchor and wings, but was rejected. Further designs submitted to the Admiralty by other artists also did not make it through the selection process. The final design was inspired by a brooch depicting an eagle, belonging to the wife of the Director of the Admiralty Air Department, Murray Sueter. A design based on this was worked up, and as a result the RNAS received its own service emblem. The eagle motif was worn as a cap badge and on the jacket cuff (the eagle to be looking outwards on the sleeve). It would also replace the naval anchor on uniform jacket buttons and belts for RNAS personnel. With the formation of the RAF in 1918, the RNAS eagle emblem became the basis for the RAF eagle cap badge emblem with minor modifications to its detailing.

10. Rear Admiral Sir Murray Fraser Sueter CB – Naval Cap

Murray Sueter joined the Royal Navy as a boy sailor cadet in 1886 on the training ship *Britannia*, achieving the rank of lieutenant by 1896, and by 1889 he was the Torpedo Officer on HMS *Jupiter*. With a brilliant technical mind and keenly interested in all mechanical devices, he was soon identified as being suitable to be a senior engineering advisor within the Navy and was chosen to oversee the Admiralty Airship No. 1 project. By 1912 Sueter was the Director of the Admiralty Air Department, and by the end of his naval career he had reached the rank of Rear Admiral. With strong opinions concerning the benefits of aircraft use in the Navy he became a leading figure in the creation of the RNAS, pushing for many innovative ideas to be explored by the Navy from the start of naval aviation and throughout the First World War. His Captain's cap, well-worn and ingrained with marks of the sweat and grime of being worn daily in his working environment, has that very direct human feel to it. What countries has it visited? What ships, offices, hangars and workshop discussions has it witnessed? What difficult meetings has it sat through? What thoughts and ideas has it contained as it sat cowling the mind of such a determined character and innovative engineer?

11. The First Naval Aviators

George Colmore joined the Navy as a cadet in 1900 and, with a keen personal interest in aviation, had sought to achieve his own Royal Aero Club pilot's certificate in 1910. This would make him the first man in the Royal Navy to hold a pilot's flying licence, albeit personally funded and achieved rather than as an officially trained naval pilot. However, keen to explore the possibilities of flight using fixed-wing aircraft, the Royal Navy in 1911 advertised for volunteers amongst its ranks who were interested in being formally trained as Royal Naval Aircraft pilots. More than 200 personnel put their names forward, of which only four would be selected for the initial training programme. These were the chosen candidates. From left to right: Lt Longmore RN (with his dog); Lt Samson RN (on aircraft); Lt Gerard RM; and Lt Gregory RN. Their training programme would be longer than normal, as the Admiralty had selected them to train to a level such that they themselves could instruct others to follow. (Lt Gerard was serving as a Royal Marine.)

12. The First Flying Field

Opposite above: In many ways Stonepits Farm, Eastchurch, on the Isle of Sheppey, Kent, has to be considered the first RNAS flying field, even though the site was owned by aviation enthusiast and entrepreneur Francis McClean. McClean was very keen to develop and promote all aspects of flight, making two of his own aircraft available to the Navy for flying training, and also a portion of the Eastchurch airfield for the Admiralty to further this pursuit. By 1912 four hangars had been erected for naval flying use on the site. The small pencil sketch by Lt J. L. Travers RN, based at Eastchurch, not only demonstrate his artistic abilities (the horse and its leader are particularly well drawn) but are a useful visual record of aircraft activities at that time. It also reminds us, unlike today, that a camera was a rare luxury indeed, and that a sketch, for most people, was the only means of capturing a visual description of a place or event. The aircraft being towed onto the flying field by horse is an early Wright Brothers machine, again reminding us of how little time had passed between man's first manned powered flight in 1903 and the Royal Navy exploring flying for its own means.

The Isle of Grain would later become an RNAS experimental aircraft and flying field (1913) with construction and maintenance hangars for aircraft, airships and numerous other aviation-connected experiments and development projects.

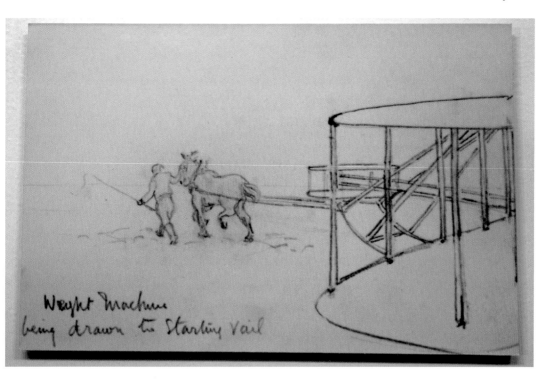

13. The First Fixed Wing Aircraft for the Navy

Previous below and above: The Short Type S.27 was one of a series of box-kite type biplanes built by the Short Bothers aircraft company in 1911, and was one of the first aeroplane types used by the Royal Navy. Based on designs proven to be successful by the pioneer aviators the Wright Brothers, the Short design would be a mainstay during the pioneer years of naval aviation. A variant of the S.27, flown by Lt Samson, performed the first take-off with an aircraft from a ship moving at sea. This historic aviation achievement took place on 9 May 1912, during the King George V Naval Review in Weymouth Bay, Dorset, with the aircraft being launched from a temporary platform fitted to the foredeck of HMS *Hibernia*.

14. Armoured Cars

Opposite above: The armoured car and the first use of an armoured fighting vehicle in the First World War can be attributed to the RNAS. Lt Charles Samson (one of the RNAS aviation pioneers) was based in France in 1914, operating his Naval Air Squadron's aircraft in support of ground forces between Dunkirk and Antwerp. With aircraft in short supply and the need for local area reconnaissance patrols becoming more vital by the day, Samson modified a Rolls-Royce Silver Ghost staff car to carry light armour plating and a machine gun. This locally produced armoured car was soon replicated with a number of officially commissioned, improved versions, constructed and modified in Royal Navy workshops. These first armoured cars, and the first armoured car squadron, proved to be of great success against light gunfire and helped pave the way for the development of many armoured fighting vehicles. The RNAS considered armoured car use to be significant enough for them to be formed into armoured car squadrons and have an official RNAS badge commissioned and issued.

15. Le Prieur Rockets

The First World War saw many new types of weaponry being developed for use on and over the battlefield. One invention, created by French Navy officer Yves Le Prieur, was a basic rocket (similar to a large firework) mounted in sets on each side of a biplane aircraft's inter-plane wing struts. The rockets (ignited by an electrical circuit and switch) were intended to be fired in one salvo towards enemy airships and observation balloons, acting as incendiary missiles. The RNAS utilised this new weapon on a number of its aircraft types and although no Zeppelins were shot down using the weapon, Le Prieur rockets proved very effective against lower altitude observation balloons over the Western Front. Although basic in its form, this was the first use of a military air-to-air missile.

16. Reginald Alexander John Warneford VC

Reginald 'Rex' Warneford was the first of only four Royal Navy pilots to date to be awarded the highest commendation for action and bravery in the face of the enemy: the Victoria Cross. Flying over Belgium in June 1915, Warneford engaged an attack on German airship LZ37. Under heavy machine gun fire from the airship, Warneford was able to outmanoeuvre the craft, climb above it and drop small incendiary bombs onto the airship, which exploded and crashed as a result. The huge explosion caused Warneford's aircraft to be overturned in flight and the engine stopped. Miraculously, he regained control and made a forced landing behind enemy lines, taking more than 30 frantic minutes to make a repair to his aircraft before taking off and flying safely back to his base. Ten days later on 17 June, and on the same day that he was awarded the *Légion d'honneur* medal by French Army officials, Warneford was tragically killed while test flying a new aircraft. His Victoria Cross, extremely rare with a blue ribbon for pre-1918 naval issue, was awarded posthumously.

17. Richard Bell-Davies VC CB DSO AFC

saw Smylie's machine burning in marshes. Landed & picked him up. Ground firm & fairly level. kept engine. He got under cowl. Returned machine climbing well. Time 10.5 - 12.20

On 15 November 1915 Lt Smiley's aircraft was struck by ground fire during a bombing mission and brought down on wasteland near Ferijick Junction, Alexandria. Alive but in imminent danger from the Bulgarian troops now racing towards his position, Smiley was spotted by fellow aviator Lt Richard Bell-Davies as he too pulled away from the area after the bombing run. Seeing the situation, and realising the peril his friend was in, Bell-Davies turned and dived towards Smiley, making a landing on the stony and rutted terrain. Now under close fire from the Bulgarian troops, Bell-Davies helped Smiley clamber headfirst into the cockpit and squeeze into the only available space in front of his feet and beneath the control panel of the aircraft. With seconds to spare and still under fire, Bell-Davies managed to again negotiate the rough terrain, get airborne and return to base safely. This was the first time that an aircraft had been used for a rescue mission, for which Bell-Davies was awarded the Victoria Cross. The second of two VC medals awarded to RNAS pilots during the First World Wat, Bell-Davies makes only a passing, casual note to this extraordinary event in his flying log book: 'Saw Smylie's machine burning in marshes, landed and picked him up.'

18. Tool Chest – First World War

To most people the image of an aircraft maintainer's tool kit would be one of spanners and an array of mechanical and metal-working devices. However, in the First World War, an aircraft maintainer's tools looked very different indeed. With aircraft construction being mostly of wood and fabric, many aircraft workers were selected from the cabinet-making and carpentry industry, bringing with them not only their skills and knowledge of high-quality woodworking and repair, but also their own specific selection of tools. Beautiful wood planes, spoke shaves, saws and chisels would travel with the individual worker in a large tool chest, usually with his name and service number hand-painted onto the outside. This precious selection of tools would be carried between airfields and squadron bases by the proud craftsman.

19. Sopwith Triplane

Opposite above: Of the many noteworthy aircraft produced and used during the First World War, one perhaps not always given the credit it deserves is the Sopwith Triplane. This was effectively a Sopwith Pup aircraft reconfigured to use the same area of wing, but split between three sets of shorter chord main planes. With an impressive climb rate, improved combat visibility and able to withstand gustier wind conditions, the Triplane would see many victories for the RNAS operating alongside the Royal Flying Corps in combat over the Western Front. The all-Canadian squadron Naval No. 10, commanded by flying ace Raymond Collishaw, claimed eighty-seven German aircraft in three months using Sopwith Triplanes. German manufacturers soon followed with their own triplane developments, again proving the success of the configuration with the Fokker Dr.1 type, a favourite aircraft of Baron Manfred Von Richthofen, 'The Red Baron'.

20. Brass Propeller Strips

An aircraft's wooden propeller can become severely damaged if large droplets of sea water smash against its leading edge while it is rotating at high speed. The splashes and droplets of water can impact the wood of the propeller with the ferocity of lumps of rock, smashing and tearing chunks from the propeller's finely honed shape, and weakening the propeller as a result. To help overcome this, most naval aircraft have the leading edges or tips of their propellers protected with a brass strip or covering. This has to be carefully carried out by the propeller manufacturer to ensure that the protective brass covering and the rivets used to fix it in place match exactly in weight on each blade of the propeller, so that the balance of the rotating propeller is not affected.

21. Short 184 No. 8359 – The Jutland Aeroplane

The Battle of Jutland, which raged over a three-day period from 31 May to 1 June 1916, saw the British and German navies engaged in a full sea battle in the North Sea, off Denmark's Jutland coast. Both sides suffered heavy damage and casualties during the combat, but significantly only one aircraft took part, a Short 184, serial number 8359. Flown by Lt Rutland (ever to be known as Rutland of Jutland) and his observer, Lt Trewin, the Short 184 was used for reconnaissance and fall of shot spotting for the British fleet, giving them a distinct advantage over the German Navy. The aircraft was preserved complete at the end of the First World War and placed in the Imperial War Museum, London. However, it was significantly damaged during German bombing raids on the city in 1939/40. The remains of Short 8359, although now much reduced, are still totally original from the time of its last flying and service use at the Battle of Jutland.

22. Squadron Commander Edwin Dunning DSC – Wristwatch

Opposite: Taking off from a ship in an aircraft had been achieved at a relatively early stage in the history of flight by Lt Samson in 1911. However, landing onto a ship moving at sea was not accomplished until 2 August 1917. This single act was a turning point for the Royal Navy and the future of how it would use aircraft. It was also a stark reminder of the dangers involved. Carrying out this precarious experiment, Dunning's first attempt to land onto a modified deck area fixed to the bow of HMS *Furious* was a success. However, with no brakes on his aircraft he relied on crew members racing out at the last second to grab the aircraft and pull it to a halt. Tragically, on his third attempt, two days later as the trials continued, his aircraft veered over the side of the ship and plunged into the sea below. Dunning's watch stopped at the time of his death, serving as a 'caught in time' reminder of just how dangerous flying from ships can be.

23. HMS *Furious* and the Tondern Raid

Following Squadron Commander Dunning's proof that aircraft could be operated from a moving ship at sea, the Navy was now keener than ever to pursue the idea of using a ship to transport and launch multiple aircraft for an attack. This became a reality on 19 July 1918 when in a joint operation RNAS aircraft and aircraft from the newly formed RAF were transported on the foredeck of HMS *Furious* to the launch position off the coast of Denmark. The subsequent raid on the German airship base at Tondern in Denmark (part of Germany at that time) would be the first attack in history by multiple aircraft launched from an aircraft-carrying vessel. With barely space to squeeze seven Sopwith Camel aircraft onto the small launch platform fitted to the ship, the successful raid paved the way for the Admiralty to press on with creating an aircraft-carrying ship with a full-length flight deck.

24. Turret-Launched Aircraft

Opposite above: Launching an aircraft from a ship moving at sea requires the aircraft to be facing into wind, and the ship to be moving forward at full speed. Depending on the wind direction, this can mean that the captain may have to deviate his ship from his desired course to achieve this – not always a timely or tactically safe manoeuvre. One solution experimented with during the First World War was to mount a launch track onto the top of a set of the ship's main turret guns, to provide a rotatable launch platform for a lightweight aircraft such as a Sopwith Pup or Camel. This could give the benefit of the ship being able to maintain its chosen course, while allowing the gun turret to be swung to an into the wind position, aiding the launch of the aircraft from its short launch pad.

25. Seaplane Lighter

Previous below: Being able to transport an aircraft many miles before launching it, thus extending its operational range, has many advantages. During the First World War the Royal Navy explored ways of moving aircraft around at sea, all of which emphasised the need ultimately for a full-sized aircraft carrier. Although only able to carry one aircraft, the Seaplane Lighter proved very successful in demonstrating the benefits of operating aircraft from offshore positions. Lighters were first utilised to transport large reconnaissance/bomber flying boats many miles further than the aircraft's expected range before launching; an obvious tactical advantage. Later versions saw a wooden deck fitted to the craft which enabled a Sopwith Camel fighter plane to be launched at sea, if towed at speed into a stiff sea breeze. Basic in its design and concept, both versions of the craft proved extremely useful against German submarines and Zeppelins at positions far out to sea. The Thornycroft-built Seaplane Lighter was the first craft ordered by the Royal Navy with the sole purpose from the drawing board of carrying an aircraft at sea – and is arguably the first purpose-built aircraft carrier. The last known remaining example of a Seaplane Lighter exists in the Fleet Air Arm Museum Collection.

26. The First Full-Length Deck Aircraft Carrier

Opposite below: By the middle of the First World War the Royal Navy had experimented with various temporary launch platforms fitted to existing ships. All of these trials were part of the series of experiments that would bring the Navy ever closer to creating what they needed to carry and operate numerous aircraft at sea. At the outbreak of war in 1914, an ocean liner (the *Conte Rosso*) lay partly constructed at the William Beardmore shipyard in Glasgow. Subsequently purchased by the Admiralty in 1916, a project was born to finish the craft with a full-length flying-off deck for aircraft. When completed, the Navy would have the world's first ship capable not only of transporting aircraft, but enabling multiple aircraft to take off and land safely on its 549-foot (167.3 m) flight deck. Equipped with workshops, under-deck hangar areas and capable of taking up to twenty aircraft, the ship, renamed HMS *Argus*, would lead the world as a new type of military ship: the aircraft carrier.

27. Trench Art

Crafting a piece of battlefield debris into an interesting or useful object or memento is an art form that has likely been around for as long as there have been battles. Popularly known as trench art in the years after the First World War, there are many examples that demonstrate the skill of those with a creative streak and access to mechanical items discarded at the end of their initial use. Aircraft mechanics and fitters would have had a ready supply of broken but interesting aircraft parts to inspire their imagination. Objects such as these pieces from broken wooden propellers were typical of their work and craftsmanship.

28. Fug Boots and Balaclava

Attacking Zeppelins in the First World War required aircraft to be taken to altitudes as high as 17,000 ft (5,181 m) in an open cockpit; the ferociously low temperatures at such altitudes would be difficult and dangerous for the pilot to endure. Any exposed skin would be frozen and frostbitten very quickly unless it was coated with a thick layer of goose grease. Flying clothing was still in its infancy and largely being adapted from early forms of motorcycle and automobile clothing. Some garments were made to specification by an officer's personal tailor. Full-length sheepskin leather thigh boots, known by pilots as Fug Boots, were first developed by Royal Flying Corps Pilot Major Lanoe Hawker VC DSO, who had Harrods make him an experimental pair. They soon became an adopted pattern for both RFC and RNAS pilots during the First World War. Sheepskin Fug Boots, a leather balaclava, thick leather coat and rabbit skin gloves were the only forms of high-altitude clothing available at the time, and would be essential for a pilot to carry out such extreme missions.

29. Pigeon Box

Opposite above: During the First World War, sending vital reconnaissance messages or urgent distress signals back to Royal Naval Air Service land bases was not an easy task from an aircraft operating at considerable distance from base. Wireless Morse communication between aircraft and land was in its infancy and, where it was available, could be intermittent and unreliable. One relatively sure method of sending a message at speed was by carrier pigeon, and most aircraft operating from Britain over the North Sea would have travelled with Admiralty carrier pigeons in special transport boxes. If enemy ships or Zeppelin airships were spotted, or if an aircraft was forced to land at sea, a message attached to the leg of a carrier pigeon could be the fastest means of relaying the information back to land. Admiralty pigeon stations were set up along the east coast of Britain to cater for this need and many urgent and important messages were relayed by pigeon, some of whom were awarded animal commendations like the Dickin Medal for animals displaying bravery in service during times of war.

30. First RAF Uniform

Previous below: It may seem unusual to place an image of the first RAF uniform in a book on historical naval objects. However, the RAF was created on the joining of the Royal Naval Air Service and the Royal Flying Corps in 1918 to create a single British military aviation service: the RAF. Suggestions for such an amalgamation are referenced as early as October 1915 in articles describing the potential for cost savings of a single 'Royal Air Service'. As a result, many features of its instigation can be attributed to both the RNAS and RFC, by then well-established services in their own right. As a suggestion for a new uniform, RNAS officer J. G. Struthers DSC had identified a source of over 1 million yards of blue-grey Russian cavalry twill fabric, providing a small sample of the fabric for discussion and consideration on the eve of the formation of the RAF on 31 March 1918. With approval to proceed with a prototype uniform, which was to be made by his personal tailor, the first RAF uniform was actually born out of an input from the Royal Naval Air Service.

31. Fairey Flycatcher

The development of naval aircraft in the peacetime years immediately following the First World War was aimed more towards reconnaissance and fleet support roles than fighter aircraft types. However, the Fairey Flycatcher would fill the role of a fighter aircraft for the Fleet for a ten-year period between its introduction in 1922 and the addition of new fighter types like the Hawker Nimrod in 1932.

32. Submarine Aircraft Carrier M2

Always pushing the boundaries of new ideas and technologies, the Royal Navy introduced the concept of an aircraft-carrying submarine to its fleet in 1928. Converted from a standard M Class submarine, the deck gun was removed and substituted with a watertight hangar, able to take a small Parnall Peto spotter aircraft. Once surfaced, the submarine's hangar door could be opened, the aircraft moved out onto its launch rail, the wings spread and a take-off enabled within a matter of minutes. The conversion and initial trials were a success; however, after M2 tragically sank with all hands on board in Lyme Bay, Dorset, in 1932, further developments of submarine aircraft carriers were abandoned.

33. RAF – FAA Tie

Previous below: With the formation of the RAF on 1 April 1918, there still remained a naval wing within this central organisation, identified from 1924 as the Fleet Air Arm of the Royal Air Force. From 1925 uniform insignia changes were implemented that would see a silver anchor and laurel leaves, superimposed onto embroidered wings, to be worn on the sleeve cuffs of RAF officers serving in the Fleet Air Arm element of the service, thus officially recognising the combination of a naval element within the Royal Air Force. This situation remained until 1937, when the government and Air Ministry agreed that naval aviation training and operations differed sufficiently enough for the Royal Navy to retake full control of its flying activities, and by 1939 the Air Branch of the Royal Navy had been established. The zig-zag pattern tie that is familiar to many serving and formerly serving Fleet Air Arm personnel was originally the proud insignia of naval aircrew of the late 1920s and 1930s. While the Fleet Air Arm was (then) the naval element of the RAF, many of the flying officers held dual rank in both the RAF and the Royal Navy. The zig zag tie, which combined Navy blue with the lighter RAF blue, dates from this period and was intended to be worn only by aircrew officers holding this dual rank. Over the passage of time this rule seems to have been relaxed, and the tie's origins largely forgotten.

34. Signal Lamp and Hand Morse Signalling

Opposite below: Sending coded messages using an electrical Morse key or a signalling lamp was common within the Navy, Army and Air Force. However, sending messages this way between aircraft in flight and from aircraft to ship could be detected by others watching or listening. The Fleet Air Arm developed its own version of Morse message sending, used between aircraft flying in very close formation and when radio silence was imperative. The observer or telegraphist air gunner would use a clear movement of his flat extended hand and forearm (pivoted at the elbow) to 'strike' or 'chop' the signal to the crew in another aircraft. The arm movement, short swift movement for a dot, slightly longer slower movement for a dash, could be shown over the side of an open cockpit aircraft such as a Swordfish, or using the arm raised within a closed cockpit aircraft. Crews could become very proficient at communicating silently between aircraft using this method, sometimes for official messages and sometimes to pass silent messages between the crews in flight.

35. Observer's Plotting and Calculating Equipment

Having launched and set out on a mission, the observer has the complex and vitally important job of guiding the aircraft (and possibly other aircraft and ships) into a fighting position, spotting and reporting fall of shot fired from ships or aircraft, and gathering reconnaissance information. At sea the aircraft carrier will rarely be in the same location as when the aircraft took off. It is therefore the observer's job, with the aid of his plotting and navigation equipment, to know where his aircraft is at all times, and be able to calculate a safe route back to the ship. This could be several hours later, in poor visibility, perhaps short on fuel, in the dark or under radio silence. Calculating speed, time, distance, direction, remaining fuel load and the route back to the mother ship accurately is essential during the entire flight and becomes second nature to a well-trained observer. Over the years a variety of hand-held navigational calculation devices have been an essential and familiar part of the observer's specialist flying equipment.

36. TAG (Telegraphist Air Gunner)

Space in a naval aircraft is limited, so the crew often comprised only a pilot, observer and telegraphist radio operator. Training crew members to carry out multiple roles was therefore essential. On aircraft equipped with a rear-mounted defensive machine gun, the telegraphist radio operator would also be trained to operate the gun. This gave rise to the term TAG, or telegraphist air gunner – a position unique to aircrew in the Fleet Air Arm.

37. Tool Chest – Post First World War

Opposite below: As aircraft developed in the years after the First World War, and as wood replaced metal in aircraft construction, so the types of tools necessary to fix and maintain them changed. All Navy aircraft apprentices were required to build up their own personal complement of appropriate tools to furnish their trade. The tools, starting with a standard tool box, were issued regularly, but paid for by an automatic deduction from their monthly wage. This system ensured that the correct types and quality of tools were compiled into a set, and also that these costly tools were keenly guarded by the individual – a perfect means of tool control, a discipline vital to safe working, ensuring that no stray tools are left within the aircraft.

38. Supermarine Walrus – The Eyes of the Fleet

Designed and built by the Supermarine aircraft company, and drawing on expertise from their extensive seaplane and floatplane designs, the Walrus became regarded as one of the most useful and dependable aircraft in the Royal Navy from its entry into service in 1933. A true amphibian, it provided the flexibility to operate from land, water and from aircraft carriers, even having the capability to be side-launched from catapult trolley arrangements on cruisers and battleships. Reconnaissance, fall of shot spotting for the Fleet, communications, medical and supplies delivery, light bombing and maritime search and rescue missions were all within the capabilities of this robust and reliable biplane. No fewer than twenty-one ship's flights, squadrons and training units operated the Walrus during its remarkable, but often un-sung twenty-year period of service.

39. Battle of Britain Airfield Scramble Alarm Bell

With Germany pressing ever harder to gain air supremacy over Britain in 1940, the RAF was stretched to the limit and losing many pilots and aircraft by the day. With its own requirements and objectives to achieve, the Admiralty could also see the desperate situation that the country was facing. In response, it seconded fifty-six Fleet Air Arm fighter pilots to assist at that critical time in what was to become known as the Battle of Britain. The scene of airmen resting in deckchairs on English airfields (such as this image of Naval Sub Lt Bramah) while waiting for the scramble bell to ring was one that many Navy pilots would became familiar with in the summer of 1940.

40. Supermarine Seafire

Synonymous with the Battle of Britain, and one of the most recognisable aircraft shapes throughout the world, the Spitfire was also modified for naval use as a quick way of providing the Navy with a high-quality fighter aircraft in late 1941. The naval variant of the Spitfire, the Seafire, may not be so well known, but made a significant contribution to naval combat flying during the Second World War. With folding wings and an arrester hook to enable it to be operated from aircraft carriers, the Seafire was used in all theatres of war from Europe to the Far East. Late model Seafires were also used at the beginning of the Korean War in 1950, operating from HMS *Triumph*, continuing the use of this successful piston engine aircraft right up to the beginning of the jet age.

41. Fighter Direction Control Tricycles

Previous below: As the number of naval aircraft in the airspace over Great Britain increased dramatically during the Second World War, so an effective new means of controlling and guiding these aircraft had to be established. To teach this complicated discipline of guiding the speed, position, direction and course of several aircraft at once, the Navy Fighter Direction School came up with a brilliantly simple solution that covered the training requirement. Crucially, it needed to cost very little money and place no aircraft or pilots in any danger. The solution was adapted ice cream sellers' tricycles (acting as aircraft) to be pedalled at certain speeds (governed by gearing and a musician's metronome) following radio instructions and compass bearings, within a square 100 yards x 100 yards that represented 100 square miles of airspace. The system worked and WRNS (Women's Royal Naval Service) Aircraft Direction Control Officers were trained to a high level of competency using this wonderfully simple and safe arrangement.

42. Lt-Cdr Eugene Esmond VC DSO

Opposite below and above: Only four Victoria Cross medals have been awarded to Royal Navy pilots in the history of naval aviation to date. All were issued to men who flew and attempted missions under the most extreme conditions, and under intense fire from the enemy. On 12 February 1942, Lt-Cdr Eugene Esmond led one such mission in a bid to stop the German battle fleet as it broke cover from the French harbour at Brest and raced through the English Channel, making for the safe haven of German ports. The 'Channel Dash' as the event has become known was a demonstration of the utmost bravery and courage. Led by Esmond, six Fairey Swordfish aircraft (each with a crew of three men) set out with limited RAF fighter cover on what was now a day instead of night-time raid. All six Swordfish were shot down on the raid and only five of the aircrew survived. All aircrew received decorations and Esmond was posthumously awarded the Victoria Cross for leading the attempt to destroy the German fleet in atrocious weather conditions and while taking the full force of defensive fire from the German ships and Luftwaffe fighter aircraft.

43. Fairey Swordfish

Of all of the aircraft operated by the Fleet Air Arm, the Fairey Swordfish stands out above many. Despite its relatively slow speed and lumbering, antiquated design, the sure-footed Swordfish proved its worth many times during the Second World War in actions such as the Channel Dash and the sinking of the *Bismarck*. Arguably its finest hour was the attack on the Italian battle fleet in Taranto harbour on the night of 11/12 November 1940. Under intense fire, twenty-one Swordfish operating from HMS *Illustrious* in the Mediterranean carried out a daring and successful night-time raid. To achieve the extended range to the target, the aircraft had long-range fuel tanks fitted, but at the expense of their rear cockpit machine guns, which were removed to save weight. The surprise attack crippled the Italian fleet and prevented it from being a threat in those waters for the remainder of the war.

44. Lilly Pad

Opposite: Creating cost-effective alternatives for landing and operating aircraft at sea has always interested the Admiralty as a means of supporting or supplementing aircraft carrier uses. The Lily Pad floating airfield was one such experiment in the Second World War which looked at creating a floating landing platform that could be towed by ship to provide a temporary airstrip at sea. The Lily floating airstrip, 520 feet long and 60 feet wide, was constructed using large hexagonal steel buoyancy drums, linked together to create a flexible floating mat strong enough to take the weight of a landing aircraft. Although secretly tested on a Scottish loch and proven to work, it was never adopted for use beyond the experimental stage. The capacity for Britain to experiment with and develop many new ideas during the Second World War, many of which were never fully utilised, but all of which took time, money and resources, is remarkable.

45. Sikorsky R4 helicopter

Often considered by many to be a relatively modern invention, few people realise that the Royal Navy, along with the US Navy and US Coast Guard Service, was exploring the potential of the helicopter during the Second World War. In November 1943, eight months before the D-Day landings had taken place, experiments with the Sikorsky R4 type helicopter were being carried out in New York harbour, and from the modified rear deck of the SS *Dahgestan*, demonstrating again the Royal Navy's interest in exploring the newest forms of aviation. By 1945 the Fleet Air Arm would have its own helicopter evaluation unit and in 1947 No. 705 Naval Air Squadron would become the first all-helicopter operational Royal Navy squadron.

46. Fifi the Puttalam Elephant

The Fleet Air Arm can move its ships, aircraft and crews globally at very short notice to respond to whatever needs and challenges are being called for. This can often mean that they arrive in locations where back-up equipment may not be available locally. The Navy has long prided itself on being resourceful, innovative and able to utilise what is at hand to ensure that operations are kept running smoothly. During the Second World War, many squadrons of Fleet Air Arm aircraft were transported to India and Ceylon (now Shri Lanka) as part of the operational requirement for South East Asia. To overcome the problem of manoeuvring heavy aircraft in and around the makeshift jungle landing fields, where towing tractors were not available, local elephant owners were employed to assist in this task. One elephant, known as 'Fifi' by squadron personnel, did sterling service manoeuvring naval aircraft around on the airfield at Puttalam.

47. Corsair KD431

Previous below: Many aircraft remain in existence from the Second World War, but of these surviving examples very few remain in complete original condition. Years of well-meaning but often invasive refurbishments and repaints have seen many aircraft stripped of their original detailing or altered with the use of modern paints and materials. Residing within the collection at the Fleet Air Arm Museum, Corsair KD431 is a remarkably intact, original example of this significant Second World War naval fighter aircraft. Having undergone an extensive five-year restoration programme to remove recent paint finishes, conservators were able to expose and preserve the original Second World War paint and markings that existed beneath. KD431 is a very rare time capsule, displaying and describing in fascinating visual detail the aircraft's true history. Paintwork, markings, scratches, witness marks, accident damage and repairs all remain original as a permanent and accurate reference source of how aircraft were worked on and operated during the Second World War.

48. Robert Hamilton 'Hammy' Gray VC DSC (Royal Canadian Naval Volunteer Reserve)

Opposite below and above: It was flying Corsair aircraft like KD431 that Fleet Air Arm (RNCVR) pilot Lt Robert Hamilton 'Hammy' Gray earned his Victoria Cross medal (only the fourth to be awarded to a Royal Navy pilot to date) leading a bombing mission under intense fire, against Japanese shipping in Onagawa Bay, on 9 August 1945. Gray led his flight of Corsairs in for the successful and daring low-level attack, managing to sink one Japanese destroyer before being shot down.

49. Dummy Deck

The deck of an aircraft carrier is an extremely limited space, so performing take-offs, landings and manoeuvring aircraft within this tight area must be practiced time and time again to ensure effective results in service. Marking out a flight-deck sized area on a land-based airfield provided a first stage safe practice area to do this, known as a 'Dummy Deck'. ADDLS (Airfield Dummy Deck Landings) or practice landings could be made with plenty of space around the flight deck-marked area, allowing for errors in approach, line up and touchdown to be made. Deck movements could be perfected and pilots would be assessed as to when they had become proficient and accurate enough with landings to allow them to start landing on board a ship.

50. Deck Park and Ranged For Take-Off

Using every available inch of a flight deck is vital to provide the maximum take-off length from a carrier deck. The tight deck parking arrangement needed is unique to naval aircraft carrier operations, and is unlike any aircraft parking you will see at airfields or airports. If an entire squadron (or more) needs to get airborne then all of the aircraft have to be positioned or 'ranged' on deck together in a very specific order to allow each aircraft to move into position in turn for take-off. This intricate, interlocked parking sequence could be practiced on an airfield Dummy Deck, allowing space for errors to be made during practice sessions. Errors made within the confines of a live working flight deck invariably result in damage to aircraft and very serious injuries to personnel.

51. Nose Art

Embellishing the side of your aircraft with personalised symbols, messages or hand-painted images has never been officially encouraged in the Royal Navy. However, since the First World War the practice has been cautiously permitted, depending on the theatre of war and situation, or when it has been considered to be a beneficial boost to morale among pilots and crews. This panel, from a Mk1 Fairey Firefly aircraft attached to No. 1772 Squadron during the Second World War, humorously depicts pilot and observer crew members Chris McLaren and Wally Pritchard. Squadrons often had talented artists among their crew (such as Petty Officer Fred Stanworth, who created this work) with the skill and ability to mix and use a very restricted palette of colours, limited only to the available ship and aircraft maintenance paints.

52. Escape Map

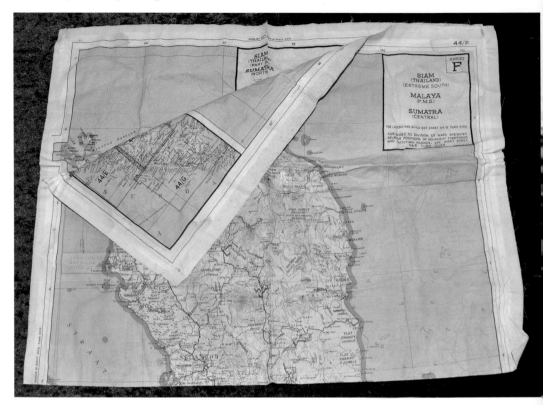

Forced landing or being shot down behind enemy lines is a silent but very real fear for any combat pilot. They will have undergone many hours learning escape and evasion tactics as part of their training. This would teach them how to hide, move and manoeuvre without being seen by the enemy, how to catch and find food, and how to navigate their way through unfamiliar terrain or countryside. One item that would be essential for an effective escape back to friendly territory would be an escape map. These maps were officially produced depicting areas over which the aircraft would be operational, and could come disguised as a large handkerchief, a silk scarf or the inner lining of a flying jacket, ready to aid an escape should the need arise.

53. Money Belt and 'Blood Chit'

Opposite: Two other items that might be carried by a pilot to aid his escape if shot down or caught in enemy territory are a money belt and a pamphlet (written in a variety of appropriate languages) clearly describing the pilot's nationality and promising payment for his safe return. The money belt (part of the pilot's survival equipment pack) would have a number of solid gold coins safely concealed into its pouch, useful to encourage any willing individual to aid the pilot's effective escape. The multilingual pamphlet (affectionately known by pilots as a 'blood chit') could be used in conjunction with the gold coins to better persuade any potential sources of assistance.

54. Vampire LZ551/G

By the closing stages of the Second World War the jet aircraft was being steadily developed by Britain, Germany, Russia and Italy. However, only four months after the end of hostilities, on 3 December 1945, the Royal Navy achieved a benchmark first in aviation history. On that day, Navy test pilot Eric 'Winkle' Brown made the historic first landing of a jet aircraft onto the deck of an aircraft carrier at sea. Manufactured by the de Havilland Aircraft Company, already famous for its highly successful Mosquito light bomber, it retained the technology best understood at that time – wood. Although the Vampire was very much a new generation, jet age aircraft with aluminium wings and twin tail booms, the whole fuselage was actually made from skilfully worked layers of plywood, covered with a cotton fabric skin and painted to keep the fuselage waterproof.

55. Captain Eric 'Winkle' Brown CBE DSC AFC FRAeS – Hanna Reitsch's Goggles

Opposite: Captain Eric 'Winkle' Brown enjoyed an extraordinary flying career in both the Fleet Air Arm and as a Royal Aircraft Establishment test pilot. He achieved a number of significant aviation firsts and flew a record number of 487 aircraft types – a record unlikely to ever be beaten. Involved in the test flight evaluation of numerous captured aircraft at the end of the Second World War, his nickname 'Winkle' (due to his small stature) would save his life on a number of occasions, with his being able to curl up tight in the cockpit space of several test aircraft that crashed on landing. Before the Second World War Eric lived in Germany as a university student, meeting with some of the significant German aviators at that time, including the female German test pilot Hanna Reitsch, with whom he regularly flew gliders as a recreation pursuit. After the war he was part of the team of specialists who were sent into Germany to select aircraft types to be captured and flown back to the UK for evaluation. It was here that he met Hanna Reitsch again, as she was being detained for questioning. Aviator to aviator, and remembering their pre-war flying days, she made a gift of her flying goggles to Eric, who kept and used them many times in his post-war flying career. What aviation history and activity have these googles shared between the flying careers of two of the world's most significant pilots.

56. RATOG

Getting an aircraft airborne within the short length of a ship's flight deck has always been a challenge, particularly as aircraft weights and payloads increased over the years. One solution adopted by the Fleet Air Arm for certain applications and aircraft types was the use of RATOG (Rocket Assisted Take-Off Gear). The RATOG equipment consisted of two very powerful rocket boosters fixed to each side of the aircraft's fuselage, giving extra power during the short take-off distance. Once airborne and clear of the ship, the RATOG boosters would be jettisoned.

57. Rubber Deck

The arrival of the new streamlined, propeller-less aircraft of the jet age offered new areas of aircraft technology to be explored. One experiment conducted by the Navy was to investigate whether an aircraft could now operate not only without a propeller, but also without an undercarriage. Heavy undercarriage components are vital for take-off and landing, but during flight take up vital space and weight-carrying capacity. If an aircraft could operate without them it would instantly increase the aircraft's fuel-carrying capacity and payload. Test pilot Eric 'Winkle' Brown successfully landed a Vampire jet with a strengthened lower fuselage onto an experimental rubber-cushioned deck in various trials between 1947 and 1949. Although successful as an experiment, there were still too many complications involved with manoeuvring an aircraft around without an undercarriage once it had landed. The experiments did, however, steer much of the thinking towards the benefits of reconfiguring a carrier to have an angled portion to its flight deck.

58. Plane Guard Helicopter

Aircraft taking off from a carrier (launching) or landing back on (recovering) have only a very small deck area to land onto. Margin for error is minimal and should an aircraft have a mechanical problem or the pilot misjudge his position, the aircraft could easily veer from the deck and plunge into the sea. In such a situation there may be only seconds to save the pilot, so during flying operations a helicopter (known as a plane guard helicopter) flies alongside the ship, ready to immediately deliver a trained medic-diver to rescue the crashed pilot. The arrival of the helicopter into service allowed the Royal Navy to develop this very specific element of Navy flying – a task which previously would have been dependant on launching a twelve-man rowing boat to assist a stricken aircraft, often with limited chance of saving the pilot.

59. Sprule Net

Opposite: The Royal Navy has always encouraged its personnel to be innovative in its thinking and be ready to put forward new and interesting ideas. One suggestion by Lt-Cdr Sprule resulted in a device being created for use beneath a helicopter to rescue people from the water. The Sprule net was in effect a fishing net set around a frame that could be lowered by winch from a helicopter and scoop up a person without having to send down a diver to aid the operation. Versions of the Sprule net are still used by some Special Forces units around the world for the fast recovery of people from both land and sea.

60. Bats

The final line-up and approach to an aircraft carrier is the most difficult and demanding moment for any pilot, and fraught with danger. Predicting the pitch and roll of the ship, and knowing if you are approaching too high or too low, is difficult to gauge from the pilot's seat alone. The introduction of a batsman on the carrier flight deck, using vivid coloured bats to indicate to the pilot what was needed to alter his position to match the position of the ship, was a breakthrough in safety and effectiveness for flight deck operations. The batsman (also a very experienced pilot) would be able to gauge the incoming aircraft's speed, height and position, and also feel the ship's pitch and roll movement beneath him. Skilfully he could combine the two and if the pilot followed his every signalled instruction, a safe landing would be achieved.

61. Illuminated Wands

As more and more flying operations are conducted in poor weather conditions and low visibility, the flight deck cloth bats needed to be substituted for a pair of illuminated wands. The principle was the same, but of course the light wands could now allow landing in a much wider range of weather and light conditions. Today, illuminated wands are still used to marshal and guide aircraft both at sea and on land airfields for low-visibility and night-time flying operations.

62. Angled Deck

Previous below and above: The flight deck of an aircraft carrier is a busy, dangerous and complicated space to work in and organise when it is in full operation. Flying operations need to be achieved quickly to be effective, with the landed aircraft parked forward, creating a clear deck space for other incoming aircraft to land. A single straight-configuration deck means that aircraft landing on and missing an arrester wire or needing to 'go around again' have nowhere to go other than into the flight deck crash barrier or the forward parked aircraft! Adding an angled section to the deck effectively separates the landing area from the launching and parking area, so that if the pilot misses an arrester wire or is forced to 'go around again' there is nothing in his way. The Royal Navy's invention of the angled flight deck solved this dual problem in a single redesign of the deck space.

63. Tractors and Tugs

Moving aircraft within hangar spaces and on carrier flight decks for many years relied on manpower to quite literally gather around and push on any sturdy part of the aircraft's structure. As aircraft carrier flight decks became ever more crowded, and as aircraft became larger and heavier, so the use of flight deck tractors or 'Tugs' became necessary. Many types of tractor have been utilised over the years, some adapted from agricultural tractor types and some specifically designed for airfield or aircraft carrier use. Controlling an aircraft on a pitching and rolling flight deck, particularly when wet and slippery, requires weight and power, so flight deck tugs are fabricated from vast blocks of steel and can weigh in at more than 10 tons to enable this.

64. Holdback Device

Above and opposite above: To get an aircraft airborne in the short distance of a carrier flight deck using the catapult, it is critical that its engines are running at maximum power. However, the aircraft's brakes alone are not sufficient to restrain the aircraft while this much engine power is applied. The release and transition from stationary to harsh acceleration has to be instantaneous. As is often the case, a simple device or solution can aid the most technical of problems, and the holdback is one such device. In essence it is a simple breakable steel ring slipped over two halves of a collet, gripped around a connector on the rear of the aircraft. Or (for more powerful aircraft) a short metal bar inserted into a special connector that temporarily fastens the rear of the aircraft to the ship's deck. The aircraft may also be pulled up at an angle to increase the angle of attack, creating greater lift during take-off. The bar has a reduced central diameter designed to hold the aircraft while at full engine power, but will break and release the aircraft as the launch force of the catapult is applied. Engineered to suit each specific aircraft type, a new holdback would be required for every aircraft launch. One can only wonder at how many thousands of these snap rings or machined bars were manufactured and used during naval aircraft carrier launches from the early 1950s to the late 1970s, their use becoming redundant with the arrival of vertical take-off aircraft.

65. Jet Blast Deflectors – JBDs

Bringing a jet aircraft's engines up to full power before take-off will inevitably create a huge blast of high-energy hot air to be thrust from the rear of the aircraft. On an airfield this is not so much of a problem, but in the restricted space of a carrier flight deck this can cause serious damage or injury to aircraft or personnel moving or working in the area behind a jet ranged for launch. To overcome this problem, and to allow flight deck operations to continue safely behind a running aircraft, large metal plates are raised to deflect the hot engine blast. These deflector plates form part of the flight deck surface when not needed, being raised into position during launch sequences only. Jet blast deflectors are a simple and obvious solution to the problem, but form an essential part of a carrier deck's fixtures and fittings.

66. Steam Catapult

Launching an aircraft from a ship at sea has always been key to how useful and effective it would be to the Navy. Unlike airfields, ships have limited space and length in which to allow an aircraft to take off. To overcome this constraint a powerful catapult arrangement has often been employed to boost the aircraft (along with its own engine power) to a speed that will allow it to leave the ship's deck fast enough to maintain flying speed. Earlier devices relied on various types of hydraulic trolley arrangements, culminating ultimately in another Royal Navy invention: the flight deck steam catapult. This utilised a track embedded into the ship's deck, carrying a shuttle, powered by steam pistons. The shuttle was connected to the aircraft via a loop of immensely strong cable. Steam generated from the ship's engines powered the pistons, thrusting the shuttle forward, taking the aircraft from standstill to flying speed in a matter of seconds and hurling it forward from the ship's deck. As the aircraft leaves the deck the launch cable slips away from its retaining hooks, being caught for re-use. Such acceleration can be so severe that pilots can black out for a split second until they get used to the experience.

67 and 68. 'Hook Down, Wheels Down'– The Arrester Hook and Cable

Above and overleaf: Landing onto the deck of a carrier requires the aircraft to be brought from flying speed to a halt in a very short distance, and the aircraft's brakes alone are not powerful enough to do this. An immensely strong metal hook, an arrester hook, attached to the rear of the aircraft by a strong metal arm, is lowered during the approach to land. This hook has to catch one of the arrestor cables stretched across the ship's flight deck, and haul the aircraft to an abrupt stop. The arrestor hook, or deck-hook as it is often known, is arguably the one single object that is a unique and defining symbol of naval aviation. Until the creation of aircraft able to land vertically, the arrester hook was the only safe way to bring a landing aircraft to a halt within the confines of an aircraft carrier deck.

The corresponding arrestor cable, the component that the hook engages with to arrest the landing aircraft, is an intricately wound combination of wires and fibrous cords, able to take the rigours and punishment of hauling an aircraft to a halt time after time. The cables, approximately 2 inches (50 mm) in diameter, are connected to powerful shock-absorbing damping devices fitted on each side of the ship below the deck surface.

69. Crash Barrier

With early versions looking like an enormous badminton court net made from large high tensile steel cables, and later designs using vertical bands of very strong woven webbing, a flight deck crash barrier is obvious from its description. Raised on powerful hydraulic rams and controlled by a skilled operator, the crash barrier is deployed as a safety device to separate aircraft landing at the rear of the carrier from aircraft and engineering teams situated at the forward end of the deck. Once an aircraft has landed safely the barrier is lowered to allow the aircraft to taxi over it and into the forward deck-park space, then immediately raised again for the next inbound aircraft. Operating the crash barrier may look simple, but with timings as tight as 15–20 seconds between incoming aircraft landing on and taxiing forward, it is critical that the barrier operator is able to gauge and judge accurately the raising and lowering to ensure that serious accidents are avoided. Should a landing aircraft misjudge its touchdown position, fail to hook an arrester cable or have a brake failure, then the crash barrier will hopefully prevent the aircraft from charging forward and crashing into the people and aircraft crowded in the forward deck space.

70. Mirror Landing Sight

As aircraft speeds increased in the post-Second World War jet age, so too did the corresponding landing speeds of the aircraft. This meant that the reaction time between flight deck batsman and pilot could no longer be relied upon to conduct a safe landing. The mirror landing sight, invented by the Royal Navy to overcome this problem, consisted of a large concave mirror (situated on the port side of the flight deck, visible to the approaching aircraft) with rows of green lights extending out each side of the mirror at the horizontal centre. A target light (fixed to the ship) would be directed into the centre of the mirror (in line with the rows of green lights). As the aircraft approached, due to the curvature of the mirror, the target light would appear above the position of the horizontal green lights if the pilot was too high, or below the green light line if too low. Assisted by radio with other direction and speed information from the Landing Safety Officer, the pilot could better judge his position and approach to the deck using this relatively simple visual aid. Later developments would dispense with the mirror and utilise banks of lights with special lenses that exposed the lights to the pilot's view (indicating high, low or correct) depending on the approach position.

71. Steering Arm

Opposite above: To achieve very tight flight deck and hangar parking, it may be necessary to disconnect the tow vehicle and its large tow bar, and replace it with a hand-controlled steering arm. This requires a team of deck personnel to gather around the aircraft in order to push the aircraft manually while the aircraft handler nimbly swings the hand-operated steering arm from side to side as appropriate, to steer an aircraft precisely into place. A skilled handler can guide aircraft into position only inches apart, maximising deck or hangar space, but never causing the aircraft to collide.

72. Aircraft Wheel Chock

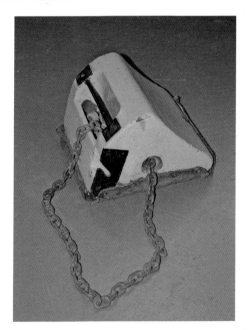

A chock is essential to hold an aircraft steady in place when parked. Basic in its design, and carried daily by aircraft handlers, yet how many people stop to notice how each part of the chock does actually have a specific purpose? From its bright yellow hi-vis colouring, its heavy, hardwood construction, specific shape, a high-friction grip-enabling undersurface, a chain to lock a pair of chocks together around an aircraft wheel, a stowage slot for the chain when not in use and a handle for the deck crew to carry it by, the humble chock is a complete design exercise and a well thought through and essential piece of aircraft equipment.

73. Flight Deck Crane

There are times when an aircraft can crash and be so badly damaged on a carrier deck that it blocks all other aircraft from landing – a blacked flight deck situation. Commander Air and the deck crews may have only seconds to check that the crew has been safely recovered from the wreckage, and decide whether to drag the stricken aircraft to one side, or maybe even dump the aircraft overboard to clear the flight deck. This latter choice would be a last resort and only exercised if other inbound aircraft were in immediate danger themselves (damaged, short on fuel, injured crew, etc.) and needing an urgent landing space. To deal with such situations, a large crane (invariably nicknamed Jumbo) would be part of the flight deck equipment, always on standby and ready to operate during flying stations.

74. Flyco

Opposite: The nerve centre of all air operations on board an aircraft carrier is the Flying Control room – Flyco. This control room is positioned high on the carrier's island superstructure, usually jutting out over the flight deck to allow maximum vison over what is happening on deck at all times. Present in Flyco would be Commander Air, Lt-Cdr Flying and other appropriate personnel to monitor and oversee the flying programme and operations.

75. *Flight Deck* Magazine

The appropriately named *Flight Deck* magazine is the monthly journal of the Fleet Air Arm. First printed in August 1944, it is still in print today. Containing naval and squadron news, updates, notifications, awards, safety bulletins and items of interest and humour, *Flight Deck* magazine has been popularly received since its inception. Distributed throughout the Fleet Air Arm as an official, censored document, early editions contained a central inserted section (paged in Roman numerals) that relayed up-to-date ship and squadron activities and movements. Versions of the magazine intended for public distribution (at air displays or ship open days) would have the central insert omitted for obvious security reasons.

76. Tugg Wilson

The Royal Navy has always attracted into its ranks a very wide range of characters, with an equally wide spread of skills and talents. Lt Cecil 'Tug' Wilson was one such character, whose ability as a cartoon artist was not only enjoyed by all personnel, but was ultimately adopted by the Navy to produce many official calendars, notices and flight safety posters. 'Tugg' became renowned for his ability to brilliantly capture the feel and expression of many situations (and people), often conveying very meaningful messages in a memorable way through humour.

77. Uckers

Overleaf above: Recreation and leisure time is an important element of squadron life, particularly when crews and personnel are away from home or at sea for long periods. Cards and board games can be a welcome distraction from the rigours of daily life and duties. Looking at first glance like an ordinary Ludo board game, the version known as Uckers is unique to the Royal Navy and Fleet Air Arm. With counter pieces often made from slices of broom handle and with complex additional rules (that can change from ship to ship or squadron to squadron), an Uckers game can last for hours (occasionally days), being carefully and preciously guarded between break periods to resume again. The basic rules of the game (now laid down in Admiralty orders) are traditionally written on the underside of the board, so should a major dispute happen within a game, the board will inevitably be 'upturned' to verify a rule, bringing the game to a natural close. Sadly, the sight of an Uckers board in a squadron crew room is now a diminishing spectacle, along with the cheering and at times impassioned debate surrounding rules and moves.

78. Deck Hockey

Opposite below: Recreational keep-fit activities on board any ship are important for the fitness, wellbeing and morale of the ship's crew, but with finite space and facilities (depending on the ship size) the range of activities can be limited. Deck hockey is one good, energetic and competitive sport that has been enjoyed by ship's crews since the days of early sailing ships, even within relatively confined deck areas. On an aircraft carrier, the deck hockey space is generous to say the least. During times of no flying, when the flight deck can be made available for recreational duties, games of deck hockey can be greatly looked forward to, with plenty of scope for inter-squadron and inter-department competition. A hockey puck might be made from a coil of rope, pouch of stuffed rags or a simple block of wood or rubber. Whatever material is used, a good supply of pucks would be needed as 'puck overboard' could be a regular occurrence.

79. The Boyd Trophy

In 1946 the Fairey Aviation Company presented Admiral Sir Dennis Boyd KCB CBE DSC with a detailed silver model of a Swordfish aircraft in recognition for his work in support of naval aviation. Admiral Boyd subsequently put the trophy forward as a yearly award, to be given to any naval pilot(s), aircrew or squadron who in the eyes of the Admiralty had excelled themselves or achieved outstanding duties within that year. The Boyd Trophy has become a prestigious and coveted award for any naval air squadron and the desire to see a squadron's name associated with it ensures that squadrons are always ready to perform to their best.

80. Ship's Cat

Cats have long been welcome aboard ships to assist in the control of rats and mice near precious food stuffs, to bring luck and to add a friendly and comforting distraction for the ship's crew on long voyages. The imaginatively named 'Puss' was the ship's cat on HMS *Eagle* during the 1950s, earning himself great respect as a mouser in and around the ship's hangars and storage areas. Puss had his own (unofficial) ID card, victualling, tobacco and rum ration cards, which he generously shared with the ship's crew! Puss earned such respect and high regard from the crew that when he sadly ended his days, in keeping with true naval tradition he was sewn into his hammock and given a full ship's burial at sea.

81. Squadron Line Book

Opposite above: All ships and naval air squadrons keep their official record books detailing and recording events and incidents for accurate future reference. These official documents are completed in a very specific manner, recording only clear, concise and relevant details. The squadron line book, however, is a much more casual document. Often taking the form of a scrapbook, it also records the activities of the squadron and its personnel, although the content is variable to say the least. Line books typically pick up on and lampoon errors, mishaps and themed jokes, mostly among the pilots and aircrew, from the humorous to the embarrassing. Line books do have some use as a reference source in much of their content, although the humour and way in which an event is portrayed is very much squadron-specific humour, and should not be relied upon to be historically accurate.

82. Flight Deck Surcoats – Greenies, Pinkies, Bombheads, Grubbers, Chockheads and Badgers...

Previous below and above and opposite above: Communication on a flight deck during flying stations has to be clear, precise and fast. Amid the cacophony of sound, much communication is done by hand signals and flags, and everyone needs to know who is who, and who is where. Deck crews therefore wear surcoats (a tabard-like waistcoat), coloured to identify each technical trade clearly, so that assistance can be summoned quickly from the right person. Developed from coloured circles painted onto the rear of an aircraft maintainer's overalls during the Second World War, the surcoat evolved into this specific item of flight deck clothing. As with many things in the Navy, nicknames soon become attached to everyday objects and situations, and the technical trades (and respective surcoats) are no exception. The original colour coding basically still applies: brown – aircraft maintainers (Grubbers); green – electrical trades (Greenies); green with blue stripe – avionics, radio, radar technicians (Pinkies); yellow – aircraft marshalling; blue for aircraft handlers (Chockheads); red with black stripe – weapons loaders/armourers (Bombheads); and white with a black stripe – mechanical engineers (Badgers). The Badgers are engineers for the ship's equipment, so part of their duty is to operate the steam catapult, hold back toggle, crash barrier, jet blast deflectors and pieces of ship's equipment that are critical for aircraft launching, but not part of the aircraft. This surcoat belonged to the Mechanical Engineer Officer No. 1 on HMS *Ark Royal* IV's last tour in the late 1970s, suitably embellished to proudly display that his team were the last 'sett' of badgers on *Ark Royal* IV before she was decommissioned.

83. Rum Ration Grog Tub

Previous below: Rum and its association with the Navy goes back hundreds of years. Originally supplied daily, along with weak beer to supplement the less than healthy fresh water supplies kept on board seventeenth-century sailing ships, the daily rum ration retained a place in daily Royal Navy life until 1970. Reduced significantly over the years from the original ½ pint per day (diluted with 2 pints of water) to ⅛ pint per day (neat), the rum ration or 'tot' remained in place more as a tradition than a necessary requirement to supplement un-purified water. With ship operations becoming ever more mechanically advanced and requiring more detailed technical focus, it was considered inappropriate to be issuing strong alcoholic drink as a regular part of the ship's daily routine. On 31 July 1970 the last daily rum tots were issued to Royal Navy personnel, and the tradition of 'up Spirits' ceased unless permitted on very special occasions with express permission from the Monarch.

84. Flying Log Book

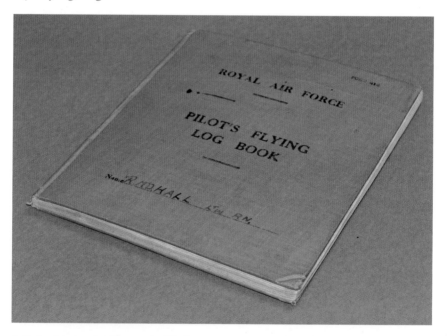

A flying log book, if correctly filled in, is a complete record of an individual's whole flying history. Every single flight, its time, location, reason, duration, the aircraft type and serial number are all briefly captured in short but accurate detail. Measuring 8 inches by 9 inches and bound in a blue cloth cover, this unassuming, standard issue Air Ministry record book (title headed RAF, but used by all services) is what most pilots or air crew would regard as their most valued possession. Some log books end up very careworn and battered, but are treasured all the same by their owners. Officially, they should be handed in to the MOD at the cessation of an individual's flying career, but most are reluctant to part with this concise document chronicling a significant part of their life.

85. Ship's Bell

All ships have a bell, used for signalling and chiming out messages and instructions to the ship's company and crew at appropriate points throughout the day. To resist corrosion in a salt water environment, as well as looking impressive when polished, ship's bells are traditionally made from brass. However, the bell on the Royal Navy's flagship aircraft carrier HMS *Ark Royal* was the only ship's bell in the fleet made from solid sterling silver. Weighing in at around 200 lbs (90 kgs) of pure hallmarked silver, the *Ark Royal* bell is arguably the most spectacular and magnificent example.

86. Dunker Training

Flying and operating over the sea brings with it the inherent danger of crashing or force landing in the water. From the earliest days of flight, the hazards and implications of this have been fully understood by all naval aviators, and since the First World War measures have been in place to teach pilots how to escape and survive from an aircraft that has had to put down at sea. Today, there is a specialist facility, with deep water tanks, wave simulation machines and simulated aircraft capsules that can be plunged into the water under controlled conditions to teach safe escape procedures. The facility is affectionately known by all pilots and aircrew as 'The Dunker'.

87. Stone Frigate

Opposite: Land-based Royal Naval bases are sometimes called stone frigates. This strange term derives from the days when out of service ships were moored permanently in a harbour as a sitting hulk, to be used as a training ship or stationary naval resource (offices, training school, stores ship, etc.). With naval air stations being developed as land-based establishments, so the name 'stone frigate' began to be applied. Fleet Air Arm shore bases usually carry two names: the geographical location name and a ship's name (e.g. Royal Naval Air Station Yeovilton is also named as HMS *Heron*). This is to enable the application of Admiralty discipline, which can only be conducted while a serving member of the Royal Navy is officially signed onto the books of a ship.

88. Sea Harrier 712½

Previous below: Superstitions have not been confined to ships and airships from the pioneer era. In the early 1990s, No. 899 Naval Air Squadron, based at Yeovilton, applied a degree of naval humour along with some determined intent to counter bad luck after two successive Sea Harrier jets coded 713 crashed within a relatively short space of time. The squadron's solution was to re-code the third replacement aircraft (ZE969) as 712½. This highly unusual and unorthodox measure is far from normal practice; however, ZE969 continued to fly with the squadron without further incident!

89. Dark Sea Grey and Sky

Fleet Air Arm aircraft colour schemes follow standards originally set by the Air Ministry, so that they comply with British military recognition and camouflage rules, as well as being compatible alongside other allied military aircraft in both combat and peacetime roles. However, one scheme known as dark sea grey and sky is unique to Royal Navy aircraft, and has been applied to many of the service's aircraft types between 1940 and 1980. A two-tone scheme, it has the dark sea grey colour covering the upper side of the aircraft and a pale grey/green colour (known as sky) covering the underside. The colours act as a camouflage against the sea in most conditions when viewed from above, while the grey/green (sky) colour blends with the numerous hazes and tones of the sky and clouds at middle to long-range distances when viewed from below. The colour scheme is also surprisingly effective against many landscape backgrounds.

90. Women's Royal Naval Service

Above and overleaf and overleaf opposite: By 1917, the impact of the First World War began to highlight an ever increasing need for people from all walks of life to fill the many necessary wartime roles within the military and in industry. To aid this, the Royal Navy created the Women's Royal Naval Service (the WRNS). Although women at that time were not permitted to go to sea or fly aircraft, their support in many other areas of naval duties provided an enormously valuable input into the war effort. Disbanded in 1919, the WRNS was reinstated in 1939 with an equally effective input into the war requirements of the Second World War, resulting in the branch being retained permanently. As the twentieth century moved on, changing social structures and workplace attitudes has seen full integration of the WRNS into all roles in the Royal Navy, including command of ships and inclusion into the naval flying training programmes. Integration has also been marked by rank badges and insignia changing from their original light blue colour to gold, now universally worn by all male and female personnel.

91. Lt Claire Donegan's Flying Overalls – First Female Pilot in the Royal Navy

Opposite and above: In 1998, aged twenty-six, Lt Claire Donegan became the first female aviator to qualify as a pilot in the Royal Navy. In 2003, flying a Sea King helicopter from No. 820 Naval Air Squadron, based at Culdrose, Cornwall, Lt Donegan carried out an outstanding rescue mission, flying in atrocious conditions to save the life of an injured and stricken yachtsman off the Cornish coast. Her flying skills earned her and her supporting rescue crew the Prince Phillip Helicopter Rescue Award, awarded only for outstanding devotion to duty during a search and rescue operation.

92. WRNS Tricorn Hat

Overleaf: Originating from the seventeenth century, and being a development of a wide-brimmed hat having its side brims folded upwards to form a more triangular shape, the tricorn hat soon became popular with all levels of society, and was also became widely used as a form of military headgear. Although progressively in decline as a style by the twentieth century, the tricorn was adopted by the WRNS in 1917 as a smaller, more stylised design, and is still the service headgear of serving female Royal Naval personnel today for senior rates and officer ranks.

93. British Aerospace Harrier

Opposite above: Like the Spitfire is synonymously connected with the Second World War and the Battle of Britain, so the Sea Harrier conjures its own similar image in connection with the Falkland Islands campaign of 1982. Barely into service with the Royal Navy when the hostilities began, Sea Harriers were transferred swiftly to the South Atlantic combat zone and put into action for the first time, with devastating effect. The Harrier's speed and agility along with its vertical take-off and landing capability demonstrated a new era of jet fighter aircraft. Later joint service versions of the Harrier have also been operated by the Fleet Air Arm in other theatres of operation. The war in Afghanistan in 2001 saw Royal Navy aircraft in support of ground troops in the desert, similar in some ways to the support shown by the RNAS to troops in the desert in the First World War. British Aerospace Harrier GR9 serial number ZD433 was acquired by the Fleet Air Arm Museum when it returned from Afghanistan and left service in 2011. The aircraft has deliberately been kept as a completely uncleaned, unaltered time capsule, showing in exact detail what a modern aircraft looks like after many months of front-line combat operational service in a desert environment.

94. Sea King ZA298 – Arctic, Desert, Jungle, Sea

Overleaf: The Royal Marines are the elite amphibious light infantry fighting force that forms one of the fighting elements of the Royal Navy. Supported by the Fleet Air Arm, the Royal Marines are frequently transported into areas of operation by Royal Navy ships and aircraft. The Fleet Air Arm Commando helicopter squadrons form a significant part of this supporting role. Sea King ZA298 has an extraordinary story to tell from its time in association with Royal Marine operations in the Falklands War, the Bosnia Campaign, the Gulf War and the war in Afghanistan. ZA298 has been on the front line of the action many times, and has been hit by enemy air-to-air and ground-to-air fire on several occasions. However, this sturdy old warhorse has brought its crew home safely each time. In a notable peacetime task, ZA298 transported the Olympic flame to the centre of London to signal the start of the 2012 Olympic Games. After more than thirty years in service, ZA298 is now in the collection at the Fleet Air Arm Museum, joining a number of historic aircraft that tell the story of the Royal Marines and their close association with the Fleet Air Arm and Royal Navy.

95. RN Fleet Air Arm Uniform

Previous: Over the years, the RNAS and Fleet Air Arm uniform has followed the general uniform style of the Royal Navy, with the most obvious detail changes being restricted to the badge, sleeve or cap insignia. Emblems (mostly sleeve badges) denoting pilots, aircrew or aircraft maintenance trades have all developed with occasional changes to identify an individual's rank and seniority. With the introduction of the Royal Naval Volunteer Reserve branch (RNVR) in 1903, an additional sleeve and epaulette design was one of the more obvious changes to the uniform. The wavy braid design, identifying personnel within this temporary or volunteer element of the service, gave rise to the light-hearted term 'Wavy Navy' being used to describe them by their full-time naval service colleagues. With the outbreak of war in 1914, the newly established Royal Naval Air Service enlisted the RNVR in all ranks and positions from aircraft maintainers to pilots. Today's modern uniforms have adopted the same straight lace rank bands on jacket cuffs and epaulettes for both regular service personnel and what is now termed RNR (Royal Naval Reserve) personnel.

96. Small Ship's Flight

Operating a single aircraft from a ship has been something the Royal Navy has been engaged with since 1911. In many ways the early experiments in this pioneering period proved the effectiveness and need to have even a single aircraft operating from a ship, as well as the desire to develop the aircraft carrier. An aircraft operating from a ship that could carry a small bombload or torpedo effectively extended the range of that weapon by carrying it further from the ship before delivery. With the arrival of the helicopter into service in 1946, and the flexibility such a machine could offer, it was an obvious step to embark a single helicopter onto a smaller class ship, such as a frigate or destroyer. Operating from a small flying-off deck at the rear of the ship, helicopters from small ships' flights have supported the Navy globally with a vast range of tasks from anti-submarine duties, reconnaissance work and ship to ship communications, to assisting with anti-piracy and drug patrols and humanitarian aid evacuations.

97. Anti-Submarine Warfare

Since the invention of the submarine, the navies of the world have striven to combat these silent and deadly underwater vessels. From the aerial spotting of surfaced submarines in the First World War to the sophisticated technologies that detect a submerged submarine using sonar devices deployed from today's helicopters, the Royal Navy has led the field with many of the anti-submarine warfare (ASW) technologies. Being able to lower a sonar device into the water from a hovering helicopter is one way that a submarine may be tracked, pinpointed and attacked using depth charges or air-launched torpedoes, carried by the helicopter. ASW helicopters in today's Royal Navy can cover vast areas of sea and remain airborne for up to 4 hours at a time. This provides a significant advantage to ship protection during times of combat where submarines are present.

98. HMS *Queen Elizabeth* – A New Carrier Era

Overleaf above: At the end of the First World War the Royal Navy had seen the benefit and potential of the aircraft carrier as significant enough to have three aircraft carriers, while the remaining navies of the world still had none. The aircraft carrier was to become a fixed and proven requirement for the Royal Navy throughout the remainder of the twentieth century. Varying in numbers and size, its presence and capabilities over the years have been observed numerous times in both combat and humanitarian aid roles. HMS *Queen Elizabeth* is one of the new breed of modern supercarriers. Greater in length than London's Houses of Parliament (280 m) with a deck area larger than three football pitches and weighing in at 65,000 tons, it is the largest ship ever built for the Royal Navy. The technology inbuilt into this new twenty-first-century fighting ship, along with the modern aircraft types that it will operate, make it among the most up to date and sophisticated aircraft carriers operating anywhere in the world.

99. Lockheed Martin F.35B

It must have been difficult for the pioneer naval aviators in 1911 to even envisage and comprehend the development of aviation to the level it had achieved within their respective naval career spans. During their lifetime aircraft would exceed the speed of sound, take off and land vertically and become more sophisticated than they could have ever possibly imagined in those early years. The modern aircraft designs of today continue that technological journey and the new generation of naval fighter pursues that quest to create a combat aircraft that is at the top of its class in both performance and reliability. Made from twenty-first-century materials, bristling with the most high-tech electronic equipment and designed to be almost undetectable on radar, the F-35B fighter would have been the stuff of science fiction and make-believe to those intrepid aviators of a century ago.

100. Henry William Allingham

When he passed away on 18 July 2009 at the age of 113, Henry Allingham was the oldest surviving veteran of the First World War. Born on 6 June 1896, Henry had been alive in three centuries. Alive before the Wright Brothers had flown for the first time, and still living forty years after man had landed on the Moon, few people have witnessed such a spread of changes in world history and the history of aviation as Henry. Indeed, Henry had the potential to see all of the subjects in this book. During the First World War he was an aircraft fitter and engineer in the Royal Naval Air Service, his rank being described as Rigger-Aero, Aircraft Mechanic First Class. English artist and sculptress Genna Gearing was inspired to craft a bronze bust of Henry as a mark of respect and celebration for Henry's great longevity. The bronze bust and Henry's medals are on permanent display at the Fleet Air Arm Museum, Yeovilton, Somerset, the home of naval aviation heritage since 1964.

ACKNOWLEDGEMENTS

Fleet Air Arm Museum and National Museum of the Royal Navy Archives, the RAF Museum, the Charles E. Brown Archive (RAF Museum), Imperial War Museum, MOD images – Crown Copyright, defenceimagery.mod.uk/fotoweb OGL. National Archives, Nicola Dowding, Catherine Cooper, Barbara Gilbert, Robert Turner, Jerry Shore, Jonathon Coombes, Robin Harper, Cdr N. D. Arnall-Culliford AFC, Cdr R. Kirkwood, Lt-Cdr C. Hillard, Richard Bridges, Charles Struthers, Al Henderson, Nigel Cheffers-Heard, G. Probets, J. Hoblyn.

ABOUT THE AUTHOR

David Morris joined the Fleet Air Arm Museum as an apprentice restoration engineer in 1981. Today, after a career span seeing several position changes, he is the Curator of Aircraft, with the museum now being part of the National Museum of the Royal Navy group. During this time David has picked up a wealth of information on the Royal Naval Air Service and its development into the Fleet Air Arm. This book not only uses a broad selection of objects to define the path of naval aviation for more than 100 years, but also allows David to add in some fascinating background information, thought-provoking details and lesser known facts that bring the objects to life in an informative and interesting way.